KT-210-210

Irises

SIDNEY LINNEGAR and JENNIFER HEWITT

Cassell

The Royal Horticultural Society

THE ROYAL HORTICULTURAL SOCIETY

Cassell Educational Limited
Villiers House, 41/47 Strand
London WC2N 5JE
for the Royal Horticultural Society

First published 1990
Reprinted with corrections 1993

British Library Cataloguing in Publication Data
Linnegar, Sidney and Hewitt, Jennifer
  Irises.
  1. Garden. Irises
  I. Title II. Series
  635.9'3424

  ISBN 0-304-31853-1

Photographs by:
Maureen Foster – cover, pp. 7, 9 (top right) 12, 14, 15, 16, 19 (centre and bottom), 22, 23, 25,
26, 29 (bottom), 33, 42 (top), 44, 47,48, 50, 54, 56, 58, 62
Harry Foster – back cover, frontispiece, pp. 4, 19 (top), 31 (bottom), 34, 41, 49, 52, 60
Ray Jeffs – pp. 20, 29 (top), 37, 38, 53
Jennifer Hewitt – pp.9 (bottom right), 31 (top), 32
G. E. Cassidy – p. 9 (top left)
Nadine Earnshaw-Whittles – p. 61
Dr S. Hirao – p. 57
Ray Wilson – p. 42 (bottom)
British Iris Society Slide Library – p. 9 (bottom left)

Line drawings by Pauline M. Dean

The authors wish to acknowledge with gratitude the
assistance of other members of the British Iris Society
in the preparation of this handbook.

Phototypesetting by Chapterhouse Ltd, Formby
Printed in Hong Kong by Wing King Tong Co. Ltd

Cover: Repeat-flowering Tall Bearded irises seen in a Welsh
garden in May
Back cover: 'Caramba', a striking modern Tall Bearded iris
Frontispiece: Siberian iris 'Silver Edge', a tetraploid
cultivar with exquisite markings

Contents

Introduction

Irises are among the most beautiful flowering plants that can be grown in temperate climates. Every garden in which the owner tries to achieve interest throughout the year needs a foundation of plants of all kinds and sizes, and irises can play their part in this. We also need excitement: the garden which lacks highlights may be quietly satisfying, but most gardeners want the thrill of seeing buds opening into spectacular flowers.

The shapes of plants and flowers are important too. Irises are architectural plants, whatever their size. The spiky leaves of the smaller ones are as valuable among the low mounds and prostrate plants of the rock garden as their taller relatives in the mixed border. The three-dimensional flowers, making an impact from a distance, reward close inspection with the intricacy of their shapes and their subtle variations in colour.

Variation is, indeed, an outstanding characteristic of the genus *Iris*. The range of colour encompasses a wider spectrum than that of many other genera and is the reason why irises take their name from the Greek goddess whose symbol is the rainbow. To those seven colours can be added brown, black, and white, with intermediate shades. There are blends, bicolors, and patterned flowers where one colour is veined or stitched with another. Leaves also make their contribution, in many shades of green and blue-green, or variegated in yellow or white. In size, irises range from dwarfs of 6 in. (15 cm) or less to tall plants of 3 ft (90 cm) or more. The tiny ones can fit into niches like jewels, while others make bolder accents or dominate their surroundings.

Irises are native to many parts of the northern hemisphere, in climates ranging from near-Arctic to almost desert. They may grow in all kinds of soils or in water, in sun or in shade. Consequently, there are irises which will suit all sorts of gardens and situations and ask no more than normal care, and a few that present a challenge to the most expert grower.

A comment often heard is that irises flower for only a short period, but it is in many cases quite untrue. There are species irises which flower for several weeks or even months and breeders have

The glamorous 'Sheik', an Arilbred iris for a sunny, well drained place

THE IRIS CALENDAR

	January	February	March	April	May	June	July	August	September	October	November	December
In the garden												
I. unguicularis and cultivars	*	*	*							*	*	*
I. histrioides, I. danfordiae	*	*										
I. reticulata and cultivars		*	*									
Juno irises (hardy)			*	*								
Dwarf Bearded species and cultivars				*	*							
Intermediate Bearded cultivars					*							
Bearded species (except dwarf)					*	*						
Tall Bearded cultivars					*	*						
Bulbous Spanish and Dutch irises				*	*	*						
Pacific Coast species and cultivars					*	*						
Evansia irises (hardy)					*	*						
I. setosa and forms						*						
Siberian irises						*						
Chrysographes species and cultivars						*	*					
I. laevigata and cultivars						*	*					
I. pseudacorus, I. versicolor						*	*					
I. foetidissima and forms						*	*					
I. foetidissima seedpods	*	*								*	*	*
Spuria irises						*	*					
Louisiana irises						*	*					
Other beardless irises						*	*					
Japanese irises						*	*	*				
Bulbous English irises							*	*				
Remontant Siberian cultivars				*	*	*	*	*				
Remontant bearded cultivars				*	*		*	*	*			
Under glass												
Evansia and Juno irises	*	*	*	*	*							
Aril irises			*	*	*							
Bulbous irises	*	*		*								
Variegated foliage												
I. pallida, I. ensata			*	*	*	*	*	*	*			
I. foetidissima, I. japonica	*	*	*	*	*	*	*	*	*	*	*	*
I. pseudacorus				*	*	*						

developed hybrids which, with more flowers on each stem and more stems to each clump, have longer flowering seasons. Any reasonably modern hybrid iris should be in bloom for three or four weeks – a period which compares favourably with peonies or lupins. The flowers themselves now have stronger substance and so do not crumple at the first shower of rain. Coming on to the market are remontant or repeat-blooming hybrids, which have two periods of bloom each year if given a little extra attention, although no more than roses, for example, require. No one iris will bloom the year round, but it is easy to have, even in a small garden, a selection of irises which will provide flowers for much of the year, to complement and contrast with other plants (see calendar).

Iris unguicularis is a joy in the depths of winter

PARTS OF THE IRIS FLOWER AND PLANT

There are some specific terms for different parts of the iris which will be used in this book. If the explanation and diagrams are compared with living plants and the parts identified, it becomes easier to understand the descriptions of species and cultivars.

Figure 1 shows two types of flowers – a bearded iris on the left and, on the right, *Iris laevigata* as a representative of the beardless irises. It is convenient for gardeners to divide irises into these two main groups. The bearded irises are broadly similar, but the beardless grouping covers a number of different types, so it may be a little more difficult to identify the flower parts.

All iris flowers have three outer petals (correctly sepals), which are known as falls. They may be horizontal (flaring), or hanging, or somewhere between these two extremes, and are usually the largest and showiest parts. The inner three petals, which are called standards, are usually upright but may be horizontal or, rarely, drooping; they are generally smaller than the falls and in a few species are only tiny bristles. In the centre is the style, which is unlike that of most other flowers. It branches into three prominent

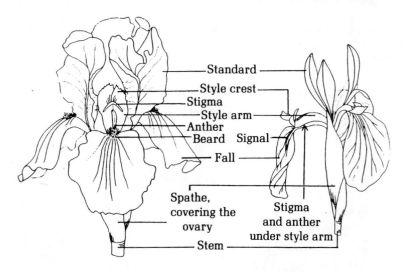

Figure 1: parts of the iris flower – bearded iris (*left*), *Iris laevigata* (right)

Opposite: different flower shapes of iris species
Above: *Iris fulva* (*left*) has hanging standards; *I. danfordiae* (right) has mere bristles
Below: the bearded *Iris variegata* (*left*); the beardless *I. ensata* (right), with small standards and wide falls

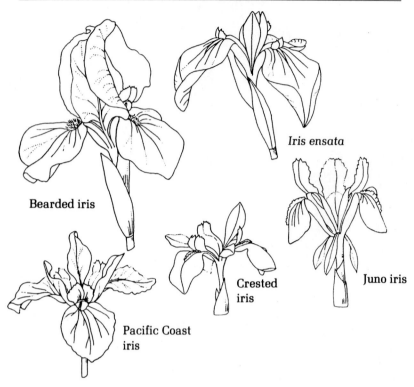

Bearded iris

Iris ensata

Crested iris

Juno iris

Pacific Coast iris

Figure 2: flower shapes of irises

petal-like arms, which arch outwards over the hafts of the falls and are often very beautifully and subtly coloured, adding to the poise and character of the flower.

Bearded irises have, on the upper parts of the falls, central bushy lines of soft hairs – the beards. These are, of course, missing in the beardless irises, which are clean-shaven, most having a patch of different colour in that area, known as a signal. The Evansia or crested irises have a ridge or cockscomb instead of a beard (see figure 2).

The rootstock of an iris includes a storage organ, which is either a rhizome that creeps horizontally along at or just below the soil surface, or a bulb 1¼–8 in. (3–20 cm) below ground level. Bearded irises are all rhizomatous, but beardless irises may have either kind of rootstock. Below the rhizome or bulb, there is usually a wide-spreading, rather shallow, fibrous root system; a few irises have spreading underground stems (stolons) as well as rhizomes and Juno irises have fleshy storage roots attached to the bulb. The

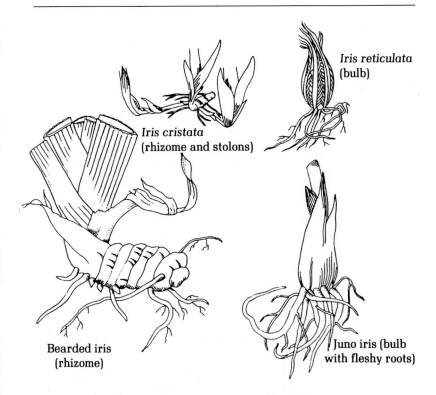

Iris reticulata
(bulb)

Iris cristata
(rhizome and stolons)

Bearded iris
(rhizome)

Juno iris (bulb
with fleshy roots)

Figure 3: rootstocks of irises

overall distinction between rhizomatous and bulbous irises is another way of dividing the genus (see figure 3).

Iris leaves vary widely in length, width and colour but grow more or less vertically. Some arch over at the tips. They grow from the centre of the bulb, or in fans from the active ends of the rhizomes.

In the following chapters, the various types of iris are described and advice is given on where and how to grow them. Where applicable, a selection of recommended cultivars is to be found at the end of the description.

The majority of cultivars in the lists, or mentioned elsewhere, are available from nurseries and others may be obtained by joining the British Iris Society. Royal Horticultural Society awards are indicated as follows – FCC = First Class Certificate; AM = Award of Merit. DM = the Dykes Medal, which is the highest award of the British Iris Society. All these awards are given after extended garden trials (unless otherwise stated).

Bearded Irises

Bearded irises fall into several sections, but may conveniently be divided into two main categories. To the first – the Pogoniris division – belong the numerous cultivars of bearded irises, grouped according to their height and flowering season. Each group has slightly different requirements for cultivation, although common factors are well drained, good soil and a sunny position. Several of the bearded species from which the hybrids are descended can be grown in the same way as cultivars of similar size.

The bearded Aril iris species and hybrids make up the second division. Most are not hardy and are difficult to grow in Britain, although a few will succeed in the right conditions.

The colour range of all the bearded Pogoniris hybrids, of whatever size, is almost the widest possible. From white it runs through yellows, orange, pink, near-reds, blues, lavender, purple and brown to black. The only pure colour not found is red, but this may be developed in time. To simplify the description of flower colours, the following classification is used:

self	single colour
bitone	different tones of one colour
bicolor	two colours (other than those below)
amoena	white standards and coloured falls
neglecta	pale blue standards and deeper-coloured falls
variegata	yellow standards and red, maroon or brown falls
plicata	white to yellow ground colour, stitched, dotted or veined in a different colour round edges of petals

MINIATURE DWARF BEARDED (MDB) IRISES

These are the first to flower, in April, and are derived from *Iris pumila* and *I. lutescens* (*I. chamaeiris*), or are throwbacks from the breeding of Standard Dwarf Bearded irises in the next group. They are charming miniatures and usually have two flowers per stem, often with open standards, giving a mass of bloom. Being almost

---

Well branched stems of Tall Bearded iris 'Annabel Jane' display elegantly ruffled flowers

stemless and only up to 8 in. (20 cm) tall, they are ideal for well drained spots in the rock garden, on the edges of raised beds and in troughs and sinks. Planted in sheltered sunny places in well cultivated soil, they soon make large free-flowering clumps. Slugs and snails are their main enemies.

There is no trial for this group at the Royal Horticultural Society's Garden, Wisley, but the lovely deep blue 'Marhaba' was given a First Class Certificate in 1971 by the Joint Iris Committee of the RHS and British Iris Society.

Like most irises, the miniatures start producing new roots a few weeks after flowering. The best time to plant or move them is between early July and September. Depending on the vigour of the clumps, they should be replanted every two or three years. Plant in groups of one cultivar, with the plants, each consisting of several linked rhizomes, 4–8 in. (10–20 cm) apart. Do not cover the rhizomes but leave the upper part exposed. Water them in and continue to water, if necessary, until they are growing well. Top-dress in spring with the mixture recommended for Tall Bearded irises (see p. 21), at a rate of 2 oz per sq. yd (60 g/m²).

Miniature Dwarf Bearded iris 'Miniscribe' (*above*), only 5 in. (13 cm) tall, and the taller Standard Dwarf Bearded 'Jeremy Brian' (*opposite*)

Cultivars

'**April Accent**' Yellow bitone, blue beard. 7 in. (18 cm).
'**Bee Wings**' Yellow with maroon markings on falls. 7 in. (18 cm). AM 1971.
'**Blue Frost**' Pale blue self, white beard. 5 in. (13 cm). AM 1968.
'**Jasper Gem**' Brownish red bitone. 8 in. (20 cm).
'**Knick Knack**' White with pale violet plicata markings. 6 in. (15 cm).
'**Orchid Flare**' Orchid-pink self, white beard. 8 in. (20 cm). AM 1971.

MEDIAN IRISES

The permanent trial of Intermediate Bearded irises at Wisley includes Standard Dwarf Bearded (SDB) and Intermediate Bearded (IB) irises. SDB irises have branched stems 8–15 in. (20–38 cm) tall, with three or four flowers per stem. The flowers should be level with, or above, the leaves. They were developed in the USA by hybridizing Tall Bearded irises with forms of *Iris pumila*. One of the

15

first cultivars, in 1951, was the still popular 'Green Spot', which received a First Class Certificate and has flowers of creamy white with, in most soils, an olive-green area around the beard.

These irises start to flower with the miniatures, in April, and continue to mid-May or later, making a delightful border edging and also being very happy in the rock garden. Cultivation is as for the Miniature Dwarf Bearded irises (see p. 14), with July the best time for planting and dividing. Space plants 8–10 in. (20–25 cm) apart.

Intermediate Bearded irises flower in May, overlapping the flowering times of Standard Dwarf and Tall Bearded irises, and are between these groups in height. The stem should be thin but strong, 15–27 in. (38–70 cm) tall, with two or more branches and at least six flowers. Those now grown have come from Tall Bearded irises crossed with Iris pumila. Iris aphylla has also been used to increase the number of flowers and give good branching on an elegant stem. 'Adrienne Taylor', blue, and 'Curlew', yellow and white, are among a number of cultivars which have gained First Class Certificates.

They can be planted 10–14 in. (25–35 cm) apart, from July to September, in similar situations to the Standard Dwarf Bearded irises, or among their Tall Bearded relations. As always, water after planting if a dry period follows.

The remaining Median irises flower in late May and June with the Tall Bearded irises. These are the Miniature Tall Bearded (MTB) and Border Bearded (BB) irises – less well known than the other groups but gaining popularity, as their height and size make them very suitable for smaller or windy gardens.

As the name implies, MTB irises are shorter versions of Tall Bearded irises, having branched, wiry, graceful stems 15–27 in. (38–70 cm) tall, which carry eight or more flowers of moderate size. Plant them 12 in. (30 cm) apart, from the end of July to September. They seem to take a little longer to settle than other June-flowering bearded irises, and need a good soil, well drained, in full sun.

The Border Bearded irises have larger, more robust flowers than the Miniature Tall Beardeds and are in the same height range, with thicker stems. They help to add variety of height to a border of modern irises. They are best given the same treatment as the Tall Bearded irises (see p. 21), and are particularly suitable for exposed positions where the latter would be blown over.

Standard Dwarf Bearded iris 'Galleon Gold', superbly situated in a rock garden

Cultivars

STANDARD DWARF BEARDED IRISES

'**Austrian Sky**' Blue self with darker blue 'thumbprint' on falls. 13 in. (33 cm). FCC 1969.
'**Bibury**' Creamy white self, blue beard. 12 in. (30 cm). FCC and DM 1982.
'**Double Lament**' Deep purple, orange beard. 12 in. (30 cm). FCC 1979.
'**Eyebright**' Rich yellow, deep maroon markings on falls. 12 in. (30 cm). AM 1978.
'**Gingerbread Man**' Rich brown self, blue beard. 14 in. (35 cm).
'**Jeremy Brian**' Silver-blue self, cream beard. 12 in. (30 cm). FCC 1984. (See p. 14.)
'**Mary McIlroy**' Deep yellow, white beard. 12 in. (30 cm). AM 1986.
'**Melon Honey**' Melon-pink self, white beard. 13 in. (33 cm). AM 1986.
'**Westwell**' Violet plicata markings on pale blue ground. 11 in. (28 cm).
'**Wow**' Bright yellow standards, maroon falls with yellow edge, yellow beard. 12 in. (30 cm). AM 1988.

INTERMEDIATE BEARDED IRISES

'**Annikins**' Deep purple-blue self. 22 in. (57 cm).
'**Arctic Fancy**' Deep violet plicata markings on a white ground, blue beard. 20 in. (50 cm). FCC 1976.
'**Chiltern Gold**' Bright yellow self. 24 in. (60 cm). AM 1972.
'**Langport Wren**' Deep red-black including beard. 22 in. (57 cm).
'**Whiteladies**' White self. 17 in. (43 cm). AM 1977.
'**Why Not**' Apricot-orange, deeper orange beard. 22 in. (57 cm).

MINIATURE TALL BEARDED IRISES

'**Aachen Elf**' Pale yellow standards, lavender falls. 20 in. (50 cm).
'**New Idea**' Rose-mulberry self. 25 in. (63 cm).

BORDER BEARDED IRISES

'**Brown Lasso**' Butterscotch standards, violet falls with brown rim. 22 in. (57 cm). DM 1981.
'**Impetuous**' Sky-blue self. 26 in. (66 cm).
'**Ouija**' Dark coppery red self. 24 in. (60 cm). FCC 1985.

TALL BEARDED (TB) IRISES

Tall Bearded irises are the showiest and best known of the bearded irises, over 28 in. (71 cm) tall, with large flowers which, nowadays,

Tall Bearded irises in a range of colours and patterns
Top: 'Gala Madrid' (left), variegata; 'Graphic Arts (right), plicata
Centre: 'Entourage' (left) and 'Rustic Cedar' (right), self colours
Bottom: 'Gold Ring' (left), bicolor; 'Dream Lover' (right), amoena

A particularly good form of *Iris pallida* grows at Tintinhull, Somerset

are usually waved or ruffled at the edges. They have been developed from hybrids between *Iris pallida* and *I. variegata*, with other bearded species involved to a lesser extent but giving essential characteristics.

Early hybrids had hanging falls like the species. However, in 1937 'White City', with flaring falls, appeared, and with 'Rippling Waters' in 1963, ruffling became the norm. The number of buds to each stem has made variable progress: 'G. P. Baker', in 1930, had 15, while in 1953, 'Headlines' had only five. Judges now expect a minimum of seven in order to ensure a reasonably long flowering period. A recent development is the remontant, or repeat-blooming, Tall and Standard Dwarf Bearded cultivars, most of which have been bred in the USA. Their performance in Britain is promising, although it depends on the weather and garden conditions.

The June-flowering Tall Bearded irises will grow and flower well in most gardens where they can be given the right position. Anyone leaving the Chelsea Flower Show may see near by a long border of vigorous bearded irises of 1930s vintage. Many well known gardens have iris borders, and there are irises in mixed plantings at Wisley and Sissinghurst Castle. Plant them at the front of a border for best results in mixed company, where their sword-shaped foliage provides contrast and variation for many months; or add spring bulbs, gladioli, crocosmias and hemerocallis to an iris bed for a succession of colour.

Like other bearded irises, Tall Beardeds prefer a well drained, sunny spot in alkaline or near-neutral soil. A pH of about 7 is best, and very limy soil must have added humus. The ground should be thoroughly dug, with old manure, spent hops or well rotted compost

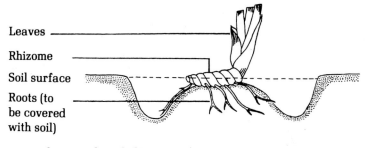

Leaves

Rhizome

Soil surface

Roots (to be covered with soil)

Figure 4: planting a bearded iris

mixed into the lower spit. None of these should be in contact with the rhizome or rot will set in. Bonemeal or hoof and horn can be incorporated into the top few inches. Established plants can be given a spring dressing, consisting of 4 parts by weight bonemeal, 2 parts superphosphate of lime, 1 part sulphate of ammonia and 1 part sulphate of potash, well mixed and applied at 2½ oz per sq. yd (75 g/m²). Alternatively, a compound fertilizer may be used, but it should not be too high in nitrogen as this will produce leaves instead of flowers. Bearded irises should never be mulched (in Britain at least) with any organic material.

The rhizomes need all the sun that our summers can provide and plants should be set so that at least the upper surface of the rhizome is above soil level (see figure 4). The only exception to this is on very light, sandy soil, when the rhizome may be planted 1 in. (2.5 cm) deep. The roots, however, should always be as deep as possible. It is important to prevent other plants, including weeds, from growing over or shading the rhizomes and to guard against slugs and snails.

Planting can be done after flowering finishes, from July to September, and single or double rhizomes are spaced about 12 in. (30 cm) apart. They will increase every year and, when the rhizomes start growing over each other, it is time to replant. Lift the clump, discard old rhizomes without growing points and any weak offsets. Dig in organic material and bonemeal as before, and plant healthy rhizomes with strong leaf fans, keeping them watered if necessary.

Cultivars

'Allegiance' Dark blue self. 40 in. (102 cm). AM 1963. DM 1964.
'Annabel Jane' Lavender bitone. 48 in. (120 cm). DM 1977. (See p. 12.)
'Black Swan' Reddish black self, brown beard. 35 in. (89 cm).
'Blue-eyed Brunette' Tobacco-brown with blue blaze on the falls. 36 in. (91 cm). FCC 1973, DM 1967.
'Broadway' Gold standards, white falls, orange beard. 33 in. (85 cm).
'Caliente' Deep wine-red self, gold beard. 38 in. (97 cm).
'Caramba' Lemon standards; white falls, edged yellow with purple plicata markings. 32 in. (82 cm). (See back cover.)
'Carnaby' Pink standards, rose-red falls edged with pink. 35 in. (89 cm).
'Cliffs of Dover' Creamy white. 42 in. (107 cm). FCC 1962.
'Dream Lover' Bluish white standards, velvety purple falls. 38 in. (97 cm). DM 1974. (See p. 19.)
'Edith Wolford' Clear yellow standards, violet-blue falls, blue beard tipped with orange. 40 in. (102 cm).

Tall Bearded iris 'Inferno', clearly showing the beard

'Flareup' Mid-brown standards, creamy brown falls, brown beard. 38 in. (97 cm).

'Jane Phillips' Pale blue self. 38 in. (97 cm). FCC 1953.

'Kent Pride' Chestnut-red plicata on yellow/white ground. 30 in. (75 cm).

'Leda's Lover' White self, pale yellow beard. 38 in. (97 cm).

'Lemon Mist' Lemon-yellow self. 30 in. (75 cm).

'Night Owl' Deep violet-black self, including beard. 38 in. (97 cm).

'Olympic Torch' Golden brown self. 40 in. (102 cm). AM 1971.

'Peach Frost' Peach-apricot standards, falls white with edging of peach-apricot. 38 in. (97 cm). AM 1985.

'Post Time' Coppery red self with beard of the same colour. 36 in. (91 cm).

'Raspberry Ripples' Rosy purple self. 36 in. (91 cm).

'Snowy Owl' Pure white with white beard. 38 in. (97 cm).

'Stepping Out' Plicata, deep purple markings on white ground. 36 in. (91 cm). FCC 1977. DM 1968.

'Sun Miracle' Brilliant yellow self. 36 in. (91 cm). FCC 1984.

'Vanity' Light pink self, coral-red beard. 36 in. (91 cm). DM 1982. (See p. 62.)

Regelio-cyclus hybrids such as 'Dardanus' are easier to grow than the Aril iris species

BEARDED IRIS SPECIES

An iris often seen in gardens is the bearded blue-purple *Iris germanica*, the old 'blue flag', flowering in May, 30 in. (75 cm) tall and almost indestructible. Many of the species have their own charm and combine well with other plants in suitable settings. *Iris pallida* is cultivated in fields around Florence, Italy, as the source of orris root, used in perfumery; it has scented, light blue flowers on 2–3 ft (60–90 cm) stems and excellent blue-green foliage (see p. 20). 'Argentea Variegata' has grey and white leaves (but undistinguished flowers), while those of 'Aurea Variegata' are striped creamy yellow with good flowers (see p. 54). *Iris albicans and I.* 'Florentina' are white-flowered, about 16 in. (40 cm) tall. *Iris variegata* (not to be confused with the variegated-leaved irises) has yellow and brown flowers (see p. 9), and the form *reginae* is white with violet veining; both grow up to 16–20 in. (40–50 cm).

Shorter bearded species include *Iris aphylla*, purple, 6–18 in. (15–45 cm); *I. lutescens* (*I. chamaeiris*), 3–10 in. (8–25 cm), yellow, purple or white; and *I. reichenbachii*, brownish purple, 7 in. (18 cm). Among the tiny ones are *Iris pumila*, usually violet-purple but sometimes white, yellow, blue or black, 3–5 in. (8–13 cm); *I. suaveolens* (*I. mellita*), 2 in. (5 cm), violet, crimson or yellowish; and *I. attica*, 2 in. (5 cm), brownish purple. The last two may do better in a frame or pot.

Bearded iris species need the same cultivation as hybrids of similar size, with good drainage, sun, and feeding as appropriate. The shorter ones should be divided and replanted frequently as they soon exhaust the soil.

ARIL IRISES

These are bearded species and hybrids from the Middle East and most will not survive the damp British winters, so must be grown under cover (see p. 52). They include the Oncocyclus and Regelia sections of the genus, which are often called Aril irises because the seeds have a white or cream appendage (aril) at one end. The hybrids between the two sections are known as Regelio-cyclus irises and may be grown outside only in the warmest and dryest parts of Britain. They have very attractive flowers with dark veining on a lighter ground.

Arilbred (AB) cultivars are hybrids between Aril irises and bearded hybrid irises. They are hardier than those mentioned above and will grow in similar conditions to Tall Bearded irises (see p. 21). Sun and excellent drainage are essential. (See also p. 4.)

Cultivars

'Lady Mohr' Standards pale lavender, falls yellow and chartreuse with crimson markings and brown beard. 30 in. (75 cm).
'Loudmouth' Dark fuchsia-red, black signal on falls. 10 in. (25 cm).
'Nineveh' Pinkish purple standards, violet-red falls. 24 in. (60 cm).

'Ancilla' Purple veining on white background, deep purple signal patch on falls. 12 in. (30 cm). AM 1957 (this award did not follow a garden trial).
'Chione' White standards, veined lilac-blue; greyish veining on falls, blackish brown patch. 16 in. (40 cm). AM 1954 (not after trial).
'Clotho' Deep violet standards, falls black, black beard. 12 in. (30 cm).
'Dardanus' Lilac standards, creamy falls veined purple. 16 in. (40 cm). (See p. 23.)
'Theseus' Deep violet with darker veins. 12 in. (30 cm).
'Thor' Purple veining, heavier on falls, on a grey background. 12 in. (30 cm).
'Vera' Reddish brown, shaded purple, blue beard. 16 in. (40 cm).

Tall Bearded irises 'Vanity', pink, and 'Jill Rosalind', white

Beardless Irises

The beardless irises comprise a very large number of species and cultivars. They include the well known Siberian and Japanese irises, Pacific Coast, Spuria and Louisiana irises, water irises, *Iris unguicularis* and *I. foetidissima*, and some less familiar species.

The cultivation needs of such a diversity of plants, from many different native habitats, are extremely varied. As a result, though, many are good garden plants, suited to different positions and conditions, and easy to grow. They can often be seen in gardens open to the public – Wisley has fine collections of Siberian and water irises, in addition to Pacific Coast irises and many species – and they are becoming more widely available from nurseries.

IRIS UNGUICULARIS

This popular iris, still sometimes called *Iris stylosa*, is valued for its flowers in winter, when it has few rivals for beauty. The scented lavender-blue blooms appear in mild spells from about November to March, borne on long perianth tubes atop short, almost non-existent stems. If the long, tough, evergreen leaves are lying flat, a clump in full flower is a lovely sight. (See p. 7.)

Iris unguicularis normally does best in a very well drained spot in full sun, preferably against a wall, but it may grow and flower anywhere in good light. Or it can fail to bloom when it seems to have everything it needs! Lime is helpful, but not essential. It resents being moved and, when division is necessary, fair-sized pieces should be replanted. Even so, it may take time to re-establish. Heavy feeding will only produce abundant leaves and no flowers. Slugs and snails love it, and birds may peck at the flowers to get the nectar. If the buds, on their perianth tubes, are gently pulled from the stems – this being the best way to pick them – they will open indoors and are lovely in simple arrangements.

Different forms include 'Alba', white; 'Walter Butt', silvery lilac, which may bloom in October; narrow-leaved 'Angustifolia', lilac-blue; and 'Mary Barnard', bluish violet. 'Cretensis' is a dwarf form

'Dreaming Yellow' is a new colour break in Siberian irises

with grassy leaves and smaller blue-purple flowers; 'Oxford Dwarf' is deep blue. A related species, Iris lazica, is native to damper habitats and is better for cooler gardens and shadier places. It may bloom intermittently from October to March, with blue-purple or lavender flowers.

PACIFIC COAST IRISES (PCIs)

There are 11 species of Pacific Coast irises, Series Californicae, three of which are not hardy in Britain. Of the others, Iris douglasiana, I. innominata and I. tenax are those most often seen and there are hybrids in almost every colour imaginable, mostly with attractive veining. Iris douglasiana has three to nine flowers on slender branched stems 6–27 in. (15–70 cm) long, in colours ranging from red-purple through lavender to blue and cream, with darker-veined falls. The long, tough, evergreen leaves are stained purple at the base. Iris innominata is smaller, with finer evergreen foliage and one or two flowers on each upright stem 6–10 in. (15–25 cm) tall. Yellow forms are commonest, but there are orange, cream, lilac, purple and blue, all beautifully veined. Of similar size, Iris tenax has one or two purple, lavender or cream flowers to a stem and may lose its lighter green leaves in winter; the similar but evergreen I. macrosiphon has scented flowers. Iris bracteata is taller and yellow-flowered, with broad deciduous leaves and bract-like leaves on the stems, a feature also seen in I. purdyi, which has cream flowers veined with purple or pink. Both are about 8–12 in. (20–30 cm) tall. All these irises flower in May and early June.

The species hybridize readily and, if several plants are close together, there will be plenty of bee-set seed, which will give a variety of hybrids. Seed or plants of these Californian Hybrids can be bought and named cultivars are also available.

Pacific Coast irises need a lime-free soil. They dislike root disturbance and it is fatal for the roots to dry out, although container-grown plants usually establish well. If they must be moved, wrap the roots in damp sphagnum moss as soon as they are lifted in September and plant them 1–2 in. (2–5 cm) deep with the moss still in place. Acid leafmould or compost should be dug in first. The easiest way with seeds is to sow three to a pot in lime-free compost. Plunge the pots in an open cold frame until the seedlings

Above: 'Banbury Pageant', one of several excellent Pacific Coast irises with the 'Banbury' prefix
Below: PC iris 'Celtic Copper' has wide falls, making it a very effective garden plant

have five leaves each, then plant in their permanent positions, which may be semi-shady or sunny, but not too dry in summer.

Cal-Sibs are hybrids between Pacific Coast irises and the Chrysographes Series (see p. 34), which flower a little later and need damper, but not permanently wet, soil. 'Margot Holmes' is red-purple and 'Golden Waves' a lovely yellow.

Cultivars
'Arnold Sunrise' White with blue shading, light orange in centre of falls. 10 in. (25 cm). FCC 1981.
'Blue Ballerina' Standards white, falls white with purple markings. 15 in. (38 cm). AM 1976.
'Lavender Royal' Lavender self with darker markings. 10 in. (25 cm). AM 1983.
'No Name' Deep yellow bitone. 12 in. (30 cm). DM 1976. FCC 1970.
Any cultivars with the prefix 'Banbury' or 'Broadleigh' are strongly recommended. (See p. 28.)

SIBERIAN IRISES

The two species in Series Sibiricae and the many well known hybrids bred from them are commonly called Siberian irises. *Iris sibirica* is deciduous, with long, narrow, arching leaves and 3 ft (90 cm) branched stems which, in June, carry six or eight blue-purple flowers, marked with gold and white on the falls. *Iris sanguinea* has shorter unbranched stems 12–30 in. (30–75 cm) tall and two or three reddish purple flowers at the level of the leaf tips. There are white forms of both species. They grow in damp meadows in the wild but do well in any good garden soil. Although they look attractive near water and prefer a moist soil, they do not like being waterlogged. Plenty of well rotted compost or manure and peat should be dug in before planting and used as a mulch in spring and autumn. When large clumps need to be divided, they can be lifted after flowering, or in September. Split them into four or five good-sized pieces and replant about 2 in. (5 cm) deep, having dug in compost or manure. Keep them watered until well established.

The same cultivation suits the named cultivars, which are descended from hybrids between the two species and their colour forms. 'Perry's Blue', 'Wisley White', 'Purple Mere', 'Helen Astor', light red, and 'Mrs Rowe', lavender-pink, are older cultivars still

Siberian irises in various forms and colours
Above: a new colour in 'Pink Haze' (*left*); 'Shirley Pope' (*right*), a study in contrasting colours
Below: 'Soft Blue (*left*), a remontant; the red-violet 'Omar's Cup' (*right*)

worth growing, with upright standards and hanging falls. In the 1950s, 'White Swirl' introduced a new flower shape, with all the petals flaring, giving a more open and flatter flower. The light blue 'Cambridge' (DM 1971, FCC 1973), and 'Anniversary' (FCC 1975, DM 1979), white with yellow hafts, have this open form and there are intermediate semi-flaring flowers such as the dark blue 'Dreaming Spires' (FCC 1974). The range of forms and colours is steadily increasing. (See also p. 26.)

Tetraploid cultivars (with twice the normal chromosome count), developed since 1970, have greater substance in flowers and foliage, richer colours and new patterns. 'Navy Brass' is deep blue with gold markings, 'Silver Edge', in lighter blue, has a white rim round the falls (see frontispiece), and there are good whites, reds and lavender-pinks.

Remontant, or repeat-blooming, Siberian irises are also being bred, mainly in the USA. They flower in May to June and again in

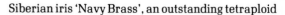

Siberian iris 'Navy Brass', an outstanding tetraploid

July, August and September. Some are performing fairly well in Britain, if they have sufficient warmth and moisture in summer, and may soon be available from nurseries.

Cultivars (in addition to those already mentioned)
'Ann Dasch' Dark blue, yellow signal on falls. 38 in. (97 cm).
'Butter and Sugar' White and yellow bicolor. 27 in. (69 cm).
'Ewen' Wine-red, tetraploid. 32 in. (81 cm).
'Pink Haze' Pink standards and falls, white style arms. 38 in. (97 cm). (See p. 31.)
'Pirate Prince' Deep blue-purple self. 28 in. (71 cm).
'Roanoke's Choice' Light lilac-pink, paler style arms. 32 in. (81 cm).
'Ruffled Velvet' Reddish purple self, yellow signal markings. 26 in. (65 cm). FCC 1989.
'Sea Shadows' Mixed blues, turquoise style arms. 36 in. (91 cm). FCC 1974.
'Soft Blue' Light blue self, possibly remontant. 30 in. (75 cm). (See p. 31.)
'Sparkling Rosé' Rosy mauve with blue flash on falls. 38 in. (97 cm).

The Siberian 'Lady of Quality' has delicately patterned falls

THE CHRYSOGRAPHES GROUP

Iris chrysographes, the species from which this group takes its name, is a good garden plant, with narrow grassy leaves and 14 in. (35 cm) stems bearing two blue, deep red-purple or, in 'Rubella', red flowers, distinguished by gold 'writing' on the falls. 'Black Knight' is a very dark form. *Iris forrestii* and *I. wilsonii* are yellow-flowered, the former 6–16 in. (15–40 cm) tall and less vigorous than the 24–30 in. (60–75 cm) *I. wilsonii*. *Iris clarkei* has 24 in. (60 cm) tall, branched stems with blue-violet flowers. The tallest is *I. delavayi*, with branched stems up to 5 ft (1.5 m) and large, deep blue-purple flowers with wide hanging falls marked in gold and white (see p. 60). All the species hybridize readily with each other and seedlings are often beautifully veined and spotted.

These irises need rather more moisture than the Siberian group and are less lime-tolerant, but otherwise require the same methods of cultivation. Flowering time is June to early July.

'Fergy's Poetry', a striking Spuria iris cultivar

IRIS SETOSA

Widely distributed in Asia and North America, *Iris setosa* usually has very small standards, which are often mere bristles, so that the flowers appear three-petalled. There are several forms, all good in the border or rock garden where the soil is lime-free and does not dry out. Taller ones are generally well branched, with up to nine flowers on 1–3 ft (30–90 cm) stems and fairly broad, deciduous leaves. Flowering is in late May and early June, and all shades of blue from lavender to deepest violet are found, as well as an albino, 'Alba'. The subspecies *hondoensis* is a particularly fine tall form with rich purple flowers.

Dwarf forms have several names, including subspecies *canadensis*, 'Hookeri' and 'Nana', and are all very similar. Their stems are about 6 in. (15 cm) tall, with one or two relatively large, lavender-blue flowers. Sometimes the standards are as large as the falls and then the flowers resemble tiny Japanese irises. They all do well in moister parts of the rock garden, with the rhizomes planted 1–2 in. (3–5 cm) deep.

IRIS FOETIDISSIMA

The Gladwyn, Gladdon or stinking iris is native to Britain and 'stinking' refers to the smell of the leaves when they are cut or bruised. It is valued in gardens for its willingness to grow almost anywhere and tolerate neglect but, if well-treated, its evergreen glossy leaves are a fine sight. The usual flower colour is a rather dingy purple overlying soft yellow, although there are bluer forms and also variants with yellow flowers, *citrina* and *lutescens*, which are more attractive. Four to seven flowers are carried on a narrowly branched, 14–18 in. (35–45 cm) stem in late June and July. Striking red or orange berry-like seeds are displayed in autumn when the seedpods split open, and remain attached through the winter, to provide colour and interest in the garden or in dried flower arrangements. Forms with white or yellow seeds are also known. 'Variegata' has green and white leaves, valuable all the year round, but is less vigorous and rarely sets seed.

SPURIA IRISES

The dwarf species of Series Spuriae flower in May or June and need well drained, sunny or slightly shaded spots, in the rock garden or at the front of a border, with the soil enriched and top-dressed with well rotted compost. *Iris graminea* makes a bold clump in semi-shade and has plum-scented purple flowers on 6–8 in. (15–20 cm) stems surrounded by fine grassy leaves. The taller variant *pseudocyperus* is unscented. *Iris kerneriana* has two to four straw-yellow flowers on 8–16 in. (20–40 cm) stems; *I. pontica* is smaller, with scented, single, lilac-blue flowers; and *I. sintenisii* forms a tufty clump of narrow leaves, the 4–12 in. (10–30 cm) stems carrying one or two white flowers heavily veined with deep violet.

Of the tall species, *Iris crocea* (*I. aurea*) is a vigorous plant with up to nine golden yellow blooms on strong 3–5 ft (90–150 cm) stems. *Iris monnieri* has frilly, soft yellow flowers and, at 16–36 in. (40–90 cm), is the same height as *I. orientalis* (*I. ochroleuca*), which has white flowers with a yellow blaze on the falls.

Iris spuria itself has six to twelve lilac-blue flowers with yellow on the falls, borne on stems 20–31 in. (50–80 cm) tall. Of its many subspecies, *halophila* has three to eight smaller, creamy yellow blooms on 16–36 in. (40–90 cm) stems; *musulmanica* (*I. klattii*), similar in height, has violet flowers with central yellow stripes on the falls; *notha* is taller, 27–36 in. (70–90 cm), with three to five deep violet flowers; and *maritima* is up to 20 in. (50 cm) tall and has creamy yellow flowers, veined purple.

The taller Spuria irises are excellent border plants for sun or semi-shade, but in cooler gardens they need plenty of sun if they are to bloom. They make large spreading clumps and must be well fed with old manure mixed with peat, or a general compound fertilizer. Plant the rhizomes 2 in. (5 cm) deep. Their main season of bloom is towards the end of June and into July.

Old hybrids such as 'Ochraurea' and the very tall 'Shelford Giant', both yellow-flowered, and 'Monspur Cambridge Blue' flower well in Britain. Many new cultivars are being bred in the USA and some are grown here, but they tend to make large clumps with few flowers. The trial of Spuria irises at Wisley will reveal those which like British conditions.

Cultivars

'Elixir' Orange-yellow. 38 in. (97 cm).
'Essay' Mauve-violet standards; falls bronze, veined mauve-violet. 38 in. (97 cm).
'Imperial Bronze' Deep yellow, fine brown all-over veining. 45 in. (115 cm).
'Protegé' Standards blue; white falls, veined blue. 38 in. (97 cm). AM 1989.
'Red Oak' Brownish maroon self. 36 in. (91 cm).

LOUISIANA IRISES

Irises of Series Hexagonae come from the southern United States and are commonly called Louisiana irises. The hardiest of the five species is *Iris fulva*, which has one or two copper-red flowers on a straight stem (see p. 9). More typical is *I. brevicaulis*, with a zigzag stem 6–12 in. (15–30 cm) long and flowers of an especially lovely blue at the top and at each joint. The hybrid between these two species, *I.* × *fulvala*, is very robust and flowers well in a bog, or in up to 4 in. (10 cm) of water, whereas the others require slightly drier conditions. All are most likely to flower in the warmer parts of Britain, so long as the evergreen leaves are not damaged in winter.

The modern hybrids from America and Australia tend to make too much leaf and flower sparsely here. They need a covering of straw in winter and feeding in spring. However, they flower fairly well if grown in large pots which stand in water 6 in. (15 cm) deep from spring to autumn. In winter, the pots are kept in a cold greenhouse and covered to protect them from frost.

'Essay', one of the Spuria irises on trial at Wisley

JAPANESE IRISES

These have been collected and hybridized in Japan for centuries and are familiarly known as *Iris kaempferi*, though the correct name is now *I. ensata*. The species typically has three or four dark red-purple flowers, with small standards and wide falls, on a 2–3 ft (60–90 cm), sometimes branching stem; the leaves have a prominent midrib (see p. 9). Cultivars with white, violet, blue, pink and red flowers and others combining two or more colours have been developed. In addition to 'single' flowers, there are 'doubles', in which the standards are as large as the falls and flare or hang down with them, and others with nine petals. 'Rose Queen' is a rosy mauve form of the species and 'Alba' an elegant white; 'Moonlight Waves', also white, has greenish tints, and 'Variegata' has striped leaves of pale green and white. Flowering in July and August, Japanese irises extend the iris season in the garden, and are also highly regarded by flower arrangers.

A Japanese iris seedling with single flowers having dark standards

Iris ensata is native to northern China and the eastern USSR as well as Japan, but it is in Japan that the species and its cultivars are held in special esteem. Great quantities are planted in public gardens and are often flooded at flowering time to increase the spectacular effect. Japanese irises do not have to be grown in water and do well planted 2 in. (5 cm) deep in any lime-free soil that does not dry out, or in a peaty bog, if fed with well rotted farmyard manure. However, they can be planted at the edge of a pond made of 'puddled' clay, in about 2 in. (5 cm) of water, when growth is particularly strong and lush. A sunny position suits them best, but they are content in partial shade.

There are many cultivars on the market and Japanese irises are now extensively hybridized in America and elsewhere, as well as in Japan. Tetraploids have been developed and remontant varieties are appearing, though they have yet to prove themselves here. It is also possible to buy seed, which can produce a range of colours and patterns; use a lime-free seed compost.

Cultivars

'Peacock Dance' Single; deep red-purple standards, falls white veined with red-violet, yellow signal, purple style arms. 42 in. (107 cm).
'Raspberry Rimmed' Single, tetraploid; standards and falls white with raspberry-red edges, golden signal. 36 in. (91 cm).
'Sorcerer's Triumph' Double; white with red-purple veining, orange signal. 42 in. (107 cm).
'The Great Mogul' Single; blackish purple self. 48 in. (120 cm).

MOISTURE-LOVING IRISES

The real water iris is *Iris laevigata*, which is happier and easier to establish at the edge of a pool than in a bog. It has two to four violet-blue flowers on 14–18 in. (35–45 cm) stems in June and July (see p. 41). Forms include 'Alba', white with touches of violet on the style arms; 'Regal', purple-red; 'Mottled Beauty', white with light blue spots on the falls; 'Atropurpurea', a deep, glowing, reddish purple; and 'Lilacina', pale blue. Perhaps the loveliest is 'Variegata', with green and white foliage which is elegant all summer, and breathtaking when the powder-blue flowers are out.

Six-petalled or 'double' cultivars have wide-open standards which are almost as large as the falls. Of these, 'Snowdrift' is white with pale violet on the style arms, and 'Colchesterensis' has white standards, and falls with deep blue centres. Darkest of all is 'Midnight', navy blue with a brilliant white line on each petal.

'Monstrosa', in white and blue, produces six or more petals and style arms which may curve horizontally, giving a whirligig effect.

Being a marginal plant, Iris laevigata does best if the roots have about 12 in. (30 cm) depth of soil mixed with well rotted manure, with water at least 2 in. (5 cm) deep over the rhizome all year.

Iris versicolor and I. virginica are native to the eastern and southern USA and similar in appearance. They will grow in any manure-enriched soil that does not dry out, or in a bog. Iris versicolor will also grow in shallow water. Well branched stems carry violet flowers in June and July, but it is a variable species with other colour forms, such as 'Kermesina', an attractive wine-red (see p. 61). Iris virginica has blue-violet flowers on an unbranched or singly branched stem. Both are 8–13 in. (20–80 cm) tall.

'Gerald Darby', a hybrid between the two species, is a very good plant for moister soil, with larger blue-purple flowers on taller stems, while 'Virginica de Luxe' has purple flowers, black stems, and red foliage in spring.

Our native yellow flag, Iris pseudacorus, is well known and a must for water gardens which have space for it to spread, although it will grow in drier places and then be less vigorous. The branching stems, 30–63 in. (75–160 cm) tall, have from four to 12 bright yellow flowers in June and July, 'Alba', white with a hint of cream, is moderate in height and vigour, as is 'Cream Form'; var. bastardii is lemon-yellow and 'Golden Queen', with larger, deep golden flowers is very vigorous. 'Variegata' is brilliant in spring and early summer with leaves striped green, yellow and cream. These usually turn all-green after flowering, but some forms remain variegated.

'Holden Clough' is a hybrid of Iris pseudacorus which thrives in damp spots. Its yellow flowers are heavily veined with brown-purple, on shorter stems, and always attract attention.

Iris pseudacorus has been hybridized with I. ensata to produce plants with quite large, bright yellow flowers elegantly veined with chestnut brown. Two named hybrids are 'Aichi-no-Kagayaki' and 'Chance Beauty'. 'Regal Surprise' is a hybrid between I. pseudacorus and I. versicolor, which has flowers with pale purple veining on a white ground, the colour being deeper on the falls. 'Limbo' is similar, but bluer. There are also lovely hybrids between I. laevigata and I. versicolor, in violet and red-purple, which are best planted in shallow water.

OTHER BEARDLESS SPECIES

Two species which will grow on limy soils in full sun are *Iris missouriensis* and *I. longipetala*. The first has a branched stem 8–36 in. (20–90 cm) tall, bearing two to five flowers of pale lilac, bluish purple or white, deeper-veined on the falls. *Iris longipetala* is shorter and the flowers have long strap-like falls. They flower in June. Both species make growth during autumn, so immediately after flowering is the time to divide and replant when necessary.

Iris ruthenica is a dwarf species with thin grassy leaves and white flowers, marked with violet, on 4 in. (10 cm) stems, from May to July. Sun or semi-shade will suit it, in a moist or dry, rich, lime-free loam, perhaps in the rock garden.

The blue-green leaves of *Iris lactea* are almost evergreen, dying down for only a short time in winter. It has two or three fragrant flowers on a 4–12 in. (10–30 cm) stem, blue-violet standards and white falls veined with blue. It does best in an open position in rich, well drained soil and can tolerate drought when established.

Iris laevigata and its white form 'Alba' make beautiful clumps at the edge of a pool

Crested Irises

The crested irises, sometimes also called Evansia irises, have distinctively flattish flowers with cockscombs, or crests, on the falls instead of beards. Some are not hardy in Britain and must be grown under glass (see p. 51). The hardy ones fall into three groups.

The first group contains some charming dwarf plants for shade or part-shade in a peat bed, or in a sink filled with lime-free peaty compost. *Iris cristata* and *I. lacustris* are stoloniferous plants native to North America, with delicately marked blue flowers, the first species about 4 in. (10 cm) tall, the second only ¾–2 in. (2–5 cm). *Iris gracilipes* is an Asian species with star-like, miniature, lilac-mauve flowers on wiry, branched, 4–6 in. (10–15 cm) stems. All these irises, and their equally lovely white forms, flower in May. September is the best time for division and replanting, and each division should consist of several rhizomes linked by their short stolons.

Two species in the second group will grow in most soils in sunny, well drained borders and need top-dressing twice a year with ¾ in. (2 cm) of rich compost. The hardiest and most robust Evansia iris is the stately *Iris milesii*: its 14–30 in. (35–75 cm) branching stems carry many pinkish lavender flowers marked with deeper purple, with a gold crest, in June. The roof iris, *I. tectorum*, needs a sheltered position and heavy feeding. The large, frilly, blue flowers have darker markings and a white crest. There is a fine white form and some good dark blue ones. 'Pal-tec', a sterile hybrid between a Pogon iris and *I. tectorum*, has silvery blue flowers.

The third group have bamboo-like stems, or canes, with fans of leaves at the top, and are less hardy. Two forms of *Iris japonica*, 'Ledger's Variety' and 'Variegata', can be grown outside in most of Britain if they have a sunny sheltered spot against a south-facing wall, in any good soil. 'Ledger's Variety' is vigorous, spreading by long underground stolons, and has short canes which look like green rhizomes. Branching flower stems up to 39 in. (100 cm) bear many pale lavender flowers marked with violet and orange. Plants must be well mulched after flowering if they are to bloom freely next year. 'Variegata' has white-striped evergreen leaves.

Above: Iris japonica has flattish flowers typical of Evansia irises
Below: Iris tectorum requires a warm, well drained spot and rich soil

Bulbous Irises

There are three groups of bulbous irises, giving colour in the garden for several months. The earliest to bloom are the Reticulata irises, which have small bulbs with net-like tunics. They are followed by the Juno and Xiphium irises, which have larger bulbs, the former with fleshy roots below them; the popular Spanish, Dutch and English irises are included in the Xiphium subgenus.

Sun and good drainage, with some moisture during periods of active growth, and summer baking to ripen the bulbs and help them produce flowers the following year, are required by most bulbous irises. (See also the Wisley handbook, *Growing dwarf bulbs*, which gives detailed cultural information and deals with Reticulata and Juno irises.)

RETICULATA IRISES

Iris histrioides, its form 'Major' and the variant 'Angel's Eye' may open their large blue flowers in January. All are reliable when they are well established. The well known *I. reticulata* has scented, deep purple flowers in February and March, and cultivars such as 'Cantab', light blue, and 'J. S. Dijt', red-purple, are similar in shape and size (see p. 50). 'George' is an excellent new hybrid of the two species, with very large, deep red flowers, and should prove hardy. Hybrids between *I. reticulata* and a related species, *I. bakeriana*, include 'Clairette', in two shades of blue, and the strongly scented, rich purple 'Jeannine'. These are robust and dependable in sunny dry positions.

The bright yellow *Iris danfordiae* has minute bristles for standards (see p. 9). After flowering, the bulbs break into tiny bulbils, which are easily lost. Planting the bulbs 10 in. (25 cm) deep in well drained, rich soil and feeding with dried blood for three years or longer may bring the bulbils to flowering size. *Iris winogradowii* has large, lighter yellow flowers and does best in a peat bed, where it should not be disturbed. All these irises have stems 1¼–2 in. (3–5 cm) tall.

A recently introduced Reticulata iris, 'Edward'

Cultivars

'Edward' Dark blue, orange ridge on falls, scented.
'Ida' Light blue, yellow ridge on falls.
'Natasha' White, tinted pale blue.
'Pauline' Purple-violet, white signal patch.
'Springtime' Pale blue standards, darker falls.
'Violet Beauty' Violet standards, deeper falls, orange ridge.
Named cultivars already mentioned are also recommended.

JUNO IRISES

The Scorpiris subgenus, usually known as the Juno irises, is a very large one, but the majority of species must be grown under glass (see p. 51). A few are generally hardy in a sunny rock garden or on a dry raised wall, except in colder areas.

Juno irises have tiny downturned standards and prominent style crests and falls. Their fleshy roots are essential for the growth of the bulb and great care must be taken not to damage them. Bulbs are sometimes sold without these roots and one way to avoid this is to buy pot-grown bulbs in flower.

An outstanding hardy species is *Iris bucharica*, which has two to six cream and yellow flowers in April on each 16 in. (40 cm) stem. An all-yellow form may be offered as *I. orchioides*. Of similar height, *I. graeberiana* has four to six pale blue flowers and *I. magnifica*, 15–24 in. (38–60 cm) tall, bears six or seven white or pale violet flowers in the upper leaf axils (see p. 48). Two hardy hybrids are 'Sindpers', greenish blue flowers, 10 in. (25 cm) tall; and 'Warlsind', yellow and blue, 10–14 in. (25–35 cm).

XIPHIUM IRISES

These irises are excellent as cut flowers and are widely sold as such. *Iris xiphium*, the Spanish iris, is a hardy species with one or two blue or violet flowers on wiry 16–24 in. (40–60 cm) stems in April or May. 'Praecox' produces its large blue flowers a little earlier and other forms are 'Battandieri', with white and yellow flowers, and 'Lusitanica', yellow. Bulbs are usually sold as 'Spanish Iris, mixed colours', although named cultivars are sometimes available. All need well drained, sunny positions where frost will not damage the leaves, which appear in early spring. Plant the bulbs 2 in. (5 cm) deep, 6–8 in. (15–20 cm) apart.

Iris bucharica, a hardy Juno which flourishes in most gardens

Iris magnifica likes a warm sunny position

Iris tingitana, 2 ft (60 cm) tall, has up to three pale blue flowers, but it is less hardy and easily succumbs to virus. Hybrids between this species and *I. xiphium* have produced the familiar Dutch iris of florists' shops, on sale for much of the year. For the garden, bulbs to flower in May and June are planted in early autumn 2 in. (5 cm) deep in sunny places; larger sizes of bulbs give the best flowers and increase faster. Treated bulbs, sold in spring for late summer flowering, are usually smaller; they will flower in August once and then, if they survive, will bloom at the normal time. The range of colours includes yellow, purple, blue, bronze and white; 'Professor Blaauw' is an excellent dark blue and 'Symphony' is white and yellow. All are about 20–24 in. (50–60 cm) tall.

Iris latifolia (*I. xiphioides*), the English iris, needs different conditions – a heavy loam in sun or part shade which does not dry out. The large bulbs should be planted 4–6 in. (10–15 cm) deep and

Iris latifolia needs damper soil than most bulbs

the same distance apart. Deep blue-purple flowers, two or three to a stem 18 in. (45 cm) tall, appear in late June or July, but wine-red, white or pale blue forms may turn up in the mixtures usually offered. Many named cultivars were available in the past and some may still be obtained from Dutch nurseries if enquiries are made.

Cultivars

DUTCH IRISES

'Blue Elegance' Purple standards, blue falls.
'Bronze Queen' Yellowish bronze.
'Duchy Blue' Violet-blue bitone.
'Lemon Queen' Yellow bitone.
'White Excelsior' White.

Irises under Glass

A number of iris species and hybrids, including uncommon ones, are tender or doubtfully hardy in Britain. They can, though, be grown successfully in a cold greenhouse, alpine house or bulb frame if given the right treatment.

The cane-type Evansias (see p. 43) will do well in a bed, or in large pots, in a cold greenhouse. Any good potting compost is suitable. They must be well fed and will make robust plants. *Iris japonica* 'Ledger's Variety' and the white-flowered *I. confusa* are both better under glass if outside conditions are unsuitable for them. *Iris wattii* has many large, almost blue flowers on 6½ ft (2 m) stems. 'Bourne Elegant' and 'Bourne Graceful' are delightful hybrids, the former having pale lavender flowers and the latter clear blue ones, all marked with deeper blue and yellow.

Tender bulbous and rhizomatous irises can be grown in a bulb frame. This is easily made by placing a cold frame on walls built of concrete blocks, two blocks high. The compost used should be a free-draining mixture, such as JI No. 3 mixed with an equal quantity of sieved coarse sand, or grit, with magnesium limestone added. Watering from below by means of perforated pipes is an advantage.

Reticulata and allied species for a bulb frame include *Iris pamphylica*, blue and brown; *I. kolpakowskiana* and *I. vartanii*, both blue and white; and *I. hyrcana*, blue. None is more than 4 in. (10 cm) tall. They will also do well in deep pans in an alpine house, as will the hardy Reticulata irises (see p. 45). Their flowers are then protected from bad weather and they may be enjoyed indoors if the pans are brought in as the flowers are about to open. 'Katharine Hodgkin' and 'Frank Elder', yellow-flowered hybrids between *I. histrioides* and *I. winogradowii*, are still expensive and are best in deep pots in an alpine house.

Juno irises are ideal for a bulb frame. They can also be grown in deep pots and, if the pot is plunged in a larger pot containing peat, the outer pot can be watered so that the neck of the bulb does not get too wet. In addition to those already mentioned (see p. 46), *Iris cycloglossa* is an exquisite species with lilac-blue flowers on simple

The hardy Reticulata 'J. S. Dijt' can equally be grown in an alpine house

The Regelia *I. stolonifera* 'Bronze Beauty' demands special care

or branched stems up to 2 ft (60 cm) tall; it may also be tried outside. Others of this fascinating group are *I. caucasica*, 2–6 in. (5–15 cm) tall with one to four yellow flowers; *I. kopetdaghensis*, with up to nine greenish yellow flowers, 10 in. (25 cm) or taller; and *I. nicolai*, 4½–6 in. (12–15 cm), with white flowers stained violet, which is a real treasure but must not be overwatered.

A bulb frame is also the best place for tender bulbs of the Xiphium subgenus, such as *Iris boissieri*, *I. filifolia*, *I. juncea* and *I. serotina*, although unfortunately these are rarely offered.

The bearded Aril irises need their own bulb frame or alpine house bed, or can be grown in pots. They must have a very gritty compost, extra feeding when in growth and good ventilation. Never overwater them and keep them completely dry from late spring to the end of autumn.

They include some of the most beautiful and exotic irises, which are far from easy to grow, but succeeding with them brings excep-

The dramatic Oncocyclus *Iris gatesii*

tional pleasure. The Oncocyclus *Iris gatesii*, 16 in. (40 cm) tall, has large whitish flowers spotted and veined grey-brown, with a deep brown signal patch on the falls. *Iris lortetii* also has large flowers, the prominent white standards veined with pink and the reflexed falls heavily marked with maroon. *Iris susiana* is greyish white veined with deep purple, 14 in. (35 cm) tall, while *I. acutiloba* is white with brownish veining and only 6 in. (15 cm) high.

The Regelia irises are slightly less demanding. *Iris hoogiana*, 18 in. (45 cm), has perhaps the purest blue flowers among bearded irises and will grow outside in a sunny sheltered spot, such as a raised bed against a south-facing wall. There is also a lovely white form. The flowers of *I. stolonifera* are a mixture of brown, purple and blue and it is 1–2 ft (30–60 cm) tall.

Hybrids between the two groups, Regelio-cyclus or Oncogelia, are hardier and easier to grow, but seem to do best in a bulb frame (see p. 25 for cultivars).

Propagation and Hybridizing

DIVISION

Named cultivars of irises can only be propagated by division, as most are hybrids which will not come true from seed.

Rhizomatous irises increase when growth buds on the sides of a rhizome develop into rhizomes themselves and then produce further offshoots. It is usually wise to leave a plant undisturbed until it has increased sufficiently to be divided into several pieces. Single rhizomes of Tall Bearded irises will establish themselves, but other bearded, and beardless, irises do better if fair-sized clumps are planted. Pacific Coast irises and *Iris unguicularis* may resent being disturbed and it is a wise precaution to lift only half the clump in one year, leaving the remainder in place, so that if the transplanted piece dies, all is not lost.

The best times for division and replanting have been given for each type of iris. As a general guide, most increase and make new roots after flowering, and can be transplanted then, but there are a few exceptions, such as *Iris missouriensis, I. longipetala* and Pacific Coast irises, which are best moved in September.

Choose strong healthy divisions for replanting and discard all dead or weak material. Large rhizomes should be cut cleanly away at their junctions with older rhizomes. Irises with short rhizomes which make crowded clumps (such as Siberian irises) can be divided by pulling them apart, using two forks back-to-back.

Bulbous irises produce bulbils at the base of the bulb and these can be grown on to flowering size *in situ*, or lifted and given special attention in a nursery bed. A clump which has many weak leaves and no flowers is in need of replanting, the bulbs being set at the original spacing after fertilizer has been added to the soil.

RAISING FROM SEED

Many iris species and hybrids can be raised from seed as easily as other perennials. Seed may be sown in autumn when it is fresh, but spring sowing is equally satisfactory.

Whether the seed is fresh or dry, it is helpful to soak it in tap

Iris pallida 'Argentea Variegata', one of several irises with variegated leaves

Above: Pacific Coast irises such as 'Simply Wild' can be tricky to divide
Opposite: Japanese irises like 'Aioi' must have lime-free conditions

water, which is changed daily, for about a week. This seems to result in a higher percentage of seeds germinating more quickly. A period of cold treatment also appears to aid germination; if frosts are not likely to occur, the seed can be put with moist peat into a polythene bag, which is placed at the bottom of the refrigerator (not in the freezing compartment) for about three weeks.

Sow the seed in drills in the open ground, or in pots using a good seed compost, with added grit for irises requiring sharp drainage. Japanese and Pacific Coast irises must have lime-free compost (see also p. 28). Except for water irises, keep the pots only just moist.

Seedlings should be pricked out when they are 6 in. (15 cm) tall or have three to four leaves. Space them 6 in. (15 cm) apart; Tall Bearded and other larger irises should be 10 in. (25 cm) apart. Plant them so that the base of the leaves is barely below the soil surface, especially for bearded irises.

Most seedlings should flower in their second or third year. When they flower, check the description, as some irises hybridize very readily with the help of bees. If the parents are hybrids, the seedlings are unlikely to resemble them closely and, in any case, they should not be called by the cultivar name of either parent.

HYBRIDIZING

Producing your own cultivars by planned cross-pollinations can be very exciting and rewarding. It is generally most satisfactory to cross two similar irises, for instance Tall Bearded × Tall Bearded or Siberian × Siberian, since irises from one group cannot be relied on to hybridize with those of another.

Select two irises, one as the female (pod) parent, one as the male (pollen) parent. On a dry day, as the flowers begin to open, remove the anthers and falls from the pod parent (see figure 1, p. 8) to prevent insects from pollinating it. Take the anthers from the pollen parent and leave them in a dry place for a few hours, until they open and the white or cream pollen grains can be seen. By this time, the stigmas on the pod parent should have bent forward, showing that they are ready to receive pollen. Holding an anther in a pair of tweezers, brush it gently along the upper surface of a stigma (the side which was pressed up against the style arm) and the deposited pollen will be visible. Repeat, using the other anthers, on the other two stigmas of the flower.

Tie a label to the stem with the name of the pod parent, followed by × and the name of the pollen parent. When the ovary begins to swell, remove the dead remains of the flower. The seed will be ripe about three months later. As soon as the pod begins to split at the top, cut it off and harvest the seeds.

Pests and Diseases

PESTS

The chief enemies of all irises are slugs and snails. Not only do they chew leaves and flowers, which is unsightly, but they cause damage through which diseases can get into the rhizomes. Dead leaves should always be removed by pulling them gently away from the rhizomes. As soon as evidence of slugs or snails is seen, or better still, before it starts, use whatever method of control you prefer.

Aphids – usually greenfly – spread virus diseases as well as weakening plants. Try to prevent any build-up by spraying as soon as they are seen, using a systemic insecticide, pirimicarb, derris or pyrethrum. If the flowers, or the hollow stems of some beardless irises, are seen to be the homes of moth larvae, spray with permethrin or pyrethrum. Iris thrips should be sprayed with malathion.

Water irises can be badly defoliated by the greyish white larvae of iris sawfly in summer. Control as for moth larvae, but not if pesticides might get into a pond or stream, when hand picking is the only solution.

Mice, voles, rabbits, even deer can and will eat rhizomes and leaves unless discouraged, or prevented from reaching the plants.

DISEASES

The commonest diseases are various rots. Bacterial soft rot can occur, especially in the rhizomes of bearded irises, if they are grown in poorly drained soil. Lengthy spells of wet weather also encourage it to develop and the bacteria often gain entry to the soft inner tissues after slugs have damaged the rhizomes. The first sign may be yellowing of the leaf tips and the whole fan may fall over, or if it is grasped, it will come away from the rhizome. The rhizome, inside its skin, is a squishy, foul-smelling, yellowish mass. Cut back the rhizome to clean white tissue and scrape the soil away from all cut surfaces. Burn all infected material, sterilize your knife and wash your hands very thoroughly, so as not to spread the rot. Then dust the cut surfaces with dry Bordeaux mixture.

Tall Bearded iris 'Sostenique', a bicolor

The 'Didcot' form of *Iris delavayi*, an example of the Chrysographes group

Leaf spot can start to appear on the leaves of bearded irises, especially in warm moist weather. Small black spots soon become larger and the leaves begin to wither. Spray with Bordeaux mixture or other copper fungicide, mancozeb or a systemic fungicide such as benomyl as soon as the first spots appear. If leaf spot has occurred before, give a preventive spray before there is any indication of trouble.

Beardless irises, especially Siberian irises, can suffer from botrytis (grey mould) in spring and summer. This is unlikely on light soils, or if they are grown with other plants. The leaf tips begin to go yellow, then brown, and grey mould can be seen at the base of the leaf fans. Spraying with benomyl, carbendazim or thiophanate-methyl will control botrytis and will also be a preventive.

Iris versicolor 'Kermesina' will grow in moist soil or shallow water

If the leaves of Reticulata or other bulbous irises start to go yellow prematurely, dig up the bulbs and examine them for black spots or streaks. These are indicative of ink disease, for which there is no cure. Dig up and burn the bulbs and any leaf remains, and do not plant new bulbs in the same place unless the soil can be sterilized first.

Irises may become infected with virus, especially iris mosaic virus, through aphid attacks or the use of infected tools. In some cases, the virus has little or no effect on the plant and may not even be suspected. But if flowers and leaves are badly deformed and striped or mottled, dig up and burn the plant, as there is at present no cure.

Index

Page numbers in **bold** refer to illustrations